The 10 Keys

On

How to Make Your Marriage Work

Vincent Hope

TANZANIA EDUCATIONAL PUBLISHERS LTD

Tanzania Educational Publishers Ltd,
TEPU House,
Uganda road, Plot No. 45 Block MDA,
Telephone: +255 685 997583/ +255 758 147871
Email: tepultd@yahoo.com
Website: www.tepu.co.tz
P.O. Box 1222,
Bukoba, Tanzania.

ISBN 978-9987-07-062-6

Dedication

This book is dedicated to My Lovely Wife

Deborah Nanchin Vincent

Whom We Have Shared This Learning Process Together

I thank the Almighty God for the Inspiration given to me

to Write this book.

Contents

Introduction

Marriage is one of the most beautiful institutions God created for the procreation of mankind and the sustenance of the earth. A man and woman are meant to come together in perfect harmony, with each person complimenting the other to achieve a common destiny. This male and female union, when properly knit together with common purpose and bonded with the belt of love, is transformed into an unstoppable force that go to great lengths and great heights together. Marriage is the core of family, the starting point and bedrock of society, when conceived, nurtured and established gives strength to families, communities, society and humanity at large.

But, to get married is one thing, and to have it last is a different thing. Marriages do break, ending up in divorce. Divorce is the worst word married people hate to hear when they get married, but, still, some marriages do break. This happens when over months, even years, they have been living together in hell instead of heaven on earth. Quarrels, hates and fights are very common when couples have trouble living together in peace. However, not all marriages are like that. There are many couples living happily together in their marriage, but, not because there is 100% absence of differences between the two, but because they have learnt how to live together happily despite the differences during the period of their marriage. They have learnt how to tame the differences and continue living together.

In this book, based on my own marriage experience, I have developed 10 Keys on How to Make Your Marriage Work.

This is a must book for all unmarried and married people.

1. Meaning and Importance of Marriage

Marriage is one of the most beautiful institutions God created for the procreation of mankind and the sustenance of the earth. A man and woman are meant to come together in perfect harmony, with each person complimenting the other to achieve a common destiny.

This male and female union, when properly knit together with common purpose and bonded with the belt of love, is transformed into an unstoppable force that goes to great lengths and great heights together.

Marriage is the core of family, the starting point and bedrock of society, when conceived, nurtured and established, it gives strength to families, communities, society and humanity at large.

This book is a story of my marriage how I have succeeded in it. It starts from the beginning, our dreams and hopes, the learning curves, the challenges, the healings, children, financial issues and so many other things that have happened in the course of our marriage.

As you read, it is my sincere hope that you will gain wisdom that will help you succeed in your marriage journey if you are already married and adequately prepare you to win if you are a young man or woman contemplating or preparing for marriage.

It is now time to enumerate and discuss the Ten(10) Keys we have adopted as a couple to make our marriage work and hopefully help to make yours work too.

Key 1: Determine to make Your Marriage Work

I grew up seeing my parents having constant quarrels and fights between themselves. It didn't happen every day or every week, but sometimes when it did happen, it got so serious that neighbours had to come around to intervene. They will shout on top of their voices, and this sometimes progressed into physical fights.

On one occasion, I was in my room and heard some noise coming from the room of my parents. I knew that there was trouble. I rushed into the room and found both of them locked in a physical battle. I went in between them to separate them.

These fights happened so often and at a point I got sick and tired of my parents and after one of the big fights they just had, I had to tell both of them that I was tired to their constant quarrels and fights. I went ahead to inquire what the reason was for these fights and off course they both accused each other of causing it.

These fights happened as a result of several issues. From lack of understanding, to inability to resolve simple matters quietly, to interference of in-laws, to lack of trust, to suspicions, to financial challenges and for several other issues.

This had a profound effect on me and I resolved that when I get married, I will make my marriage work no matter the odds. I have always had this determination in mind every step of the way in my marriage journey even until this day.

On several occasions when I had huge disagreement with my wife over issues, which dragged on for days, I always hear myself saying to myself – Your marriage must not fail- you must do everything to make it work, this disposition most times led me to apologize in order to resolve matters quickly even when I was not at fault.

One of the earliest heated debates or quarrels we had as a couple was on the issue of my mother-in-law. In my book, "The Aisle," I wrote in graphic details of all the challenges I had to surmount in order to get married to my wife. It was a difficult time for me because of the so many disapprovals and negative vibes that were coming from her.

I wrote about and incident that happened during our time of dating when she (my mother in-law) burnt the gift my wife had bought for me on my birthday. Because of this and so many other difficulties I had gone through, I vowed that she would not be welcomed at my home or be given any significant access to our home.

On this occasion, my mother in-law who served with the government as a school teacher, had exhausted her monthly earnings salary and needed some money to take care of some bills. She asked my wife for it, who at that time was not working and she in-turn asked me for the money.

At that time I saw it as a perfect opportunity to get back at her for all the hurdles she had to put me through. I gave my wife silly reasons why I should not give her mum the money, but you could see in her that she really wanted to help her mum who was seriously in need at that time.

Since that was not working, I kept lamenting on why I should not release the funds and in time, I picked up a quarrel with my wife and this turned into a heated debate which left her hurt. There was no communication between us for some time, but I knew I should not make it last longer than necessary so that it does not become ugly.

Since I started the quarrel, I had to step down from my high horse and humble myself to save the day.

I went into the room, held her and apologized.

This I did from the very basis of the mindset that my marriage must work.

When you have this kind of mindset it guides you on every issue of marriage just as it has guided me over the years.

You know that you must not allow any issue that arises in the course of the marriage to escalate to the point of no return.

This disposition will help you deescalate any issue quickly, seek room for peace and move head to have a happy home. Making up your mind that your marriage must work from the very beginning, is one key that will help you have a successful marriage.

Key 2 : Share Companionship

Marriage is first a relationship between two people before it is a medium for procreation of the humans as important as that is.

It is a company of two people who are meant to consistently relate, share, communicate and bond together.

Nothing kills marriage faster than when the two people begin growing apart which could be a result of distance caused by two couples working in different districts, states, regions, or countries, or as a result of lack of communication of both couples due to very busy work schedules in the office and both coming back late and not having time to talk or share their day's experiences.

Every time a couple communicates with each other, every time they share their experiences, their minds synchronizes, it becomes more woven together, one more thread is added to the cord that ties them together, their thinking is welded with new rods, they begin to see things the same way on a particular subject and this is when bonding happens.

As this process continues daily, the marriage gets strengthened, marriage conflicts become lesser and lesser, the love between the couple grows.

Conflicts in many marriage arise as a result of differences in opinions and points of view. When it leads to divorce, it is called **"irreconcilable differences"**.

These negative results that arise because of differences in opinions or points of view, is caused by the lack of proper understanding of concept of differences.

Let's look at the concept of a "meal".

Every woman who has ever prepared a meal or even any man who has ever been to the kitchen or has some knowledge about cooking, knows that for you to cook a good meal, you require a variety of ingredients to make it tasty.

These ingredients are different in nature and different in taste. They have to be combined in the right proportions to make a good meal. If there is too much of one ingredient e.g. too much salt or pepper, it spoils the taste of the whole meal and if an ingredient is used in less proportion, the meal does not have a great taste.

Also if only one ingredient is used to cook the meal, that meal may not be edible or it may become impossible to consume.

The same analogy can be applied to marriage. The fact that the two people involved are different is beautiful in-itself.

It is not a problem but an advantage. It should not be a source of conflict but as source of strength. When the differences between a couple are harnessed in the right proportions the marriage becomes strong. They can achieve more with less. The creator knew that a man and a woman are different in physic, nature and understanding, but still set them up together in the beautiful institution of marriage. They both complimented each other well which was perfection at work.

Conflicts arise when one of the couple, either the man or woman tries to be overbearing in the relationship, without giving much room to the other to express himself or herself, give an opinion or make a contribution to an issue. Just as too much of an ingredient in a meal spoils the taste, also if one of the couple does not make enough contributions to the marriage or does not make his or her presence felt, it can also cause problems.

The big key to a successful marriage is for both to understand their differences, appreciate them and see how to use and combine those differences to become strengths instead of becoming weakness. Differences should be a source of power rather than as source of failure.

In my marriage I realized that my wife was of the very outgoing type. She is a kind of person that strikes out an impression on a person on first contact.

She is very friendly, caring, warm and full of smiles. On the other hand, I am a very quiet person, I may not talk or relate much and can stay on my own for a long time working and not communicating with anyone.

I am not a very outgoing person and do not make much friends, not to talk of keeping them, although I have learnt so much from her.

Because of this personality of hers, she's been able to connect, build and hold on to relationships that matter in our lives', which if left to me alone would have crumbled. This is the strength she brings to our relationship.

When it comes to managing finances she is not very good at that. She is usually emotional when it comes to financial dealings and may prefer to spend money on an item on emotion rather than priority.

And that is where I come in. I am very disciplined financially, and I hold myself to account on every penny I spend. I also know how to allocate resources to deal with financial issues especially according to priority. So, when it comes to planning the home finances, she leaves much of it to me to decide.

This is where I balance out my spouse. This gives strength to the marriage such that it keeps our finances of our home on track and does not go off course.

Though we are different in makeup, skills sets and character, our individual differences have become our strength and that has helped our marriage to stay on course.

So, your individual differences don't have to be causes of quarrels, fights or irreconcilable differences but a source of strength, balance and progress.

Key 3: Grow Together

Most times the best examples of growth we see is physical growth e.g. when a plant develops from a seed to seedling into a matured tree or when a child grows from the suckling stage, to crawling, to standing and then walking and continues to increase in size i.e. grows taller.

We do not quiet notice or see the other aspect of growth which is of the mind because it is not physical. As a child grows physically, he learns new things. He learns to recognize people, hold things more firmly, eats by himself and communicates with language.

In time he or she goes to school and is taught how to read and write. He learns how to count and use numbers, recite the number times table, identify objects by their names, write sentences and this continues.

This is a mental growth that can only be seen when the person expresses it physically.

In marriage there is a lot of growth that should happen to the couple. Couples are supposed to grow together emotionally, mentally and spiritually.

Mental Growth

One of the things that kills a marriage fast is ignorance. Ignorance is simply lack of knowledge on a particular subject matter that couples have to deal with. It can range from ignorance about the needs of a man or woman, ignorance about diets or health issues, ignorance about sex or ignorance about dealing with in-laws.

A couple who do not make it a priority to learn about these issues will continue to have challenges for a long time to come.

There are so many books that have been written on a variety of these subjects which could be easily purchased. It is unwise to live in perpetual ignorance and continue to have difficulty in marriage over simple matters, when you can just pickup a book and help yourself with valuable information that can practically solve them.

My wife and I decided from the very beginning to make learning a vital part of our marriage. At every opportunity we have, we buy books on various marriage topics such as, understanding a man, understanding a woman, having healthy sexual relations, child bearing, raising children, dealing with in laws etc.

When we study individually, we discuss the vital points we have learnt from the book, share experiences on how to apply them and gain collective wisdom. We then exchange books we have read so that each of us can further strengthen the points we have discussed.

By these continuous interactions of our learning during the day, we keep on growing. This helps when one of us is going overboard on a particular subject matter, we simply remind ourselves of what we have learnt together and we retrace our steps.

For example if I start getting quite nasty or irritable or I begin to raise my voice at the children, my wife will quickly call my attention to it. We have used this method severally and it has served us well.

Couples who must succeed in their marriage must learn and grow together.

Key 4: Make yourself a better Person

We all want better wives and better husbands. When a couple has issues they failed to resolve which get out into the open, each person blames the other for their misfortune.

The husband wants his wife to change, the wife wants her husband to change, but in very rare occasions has the couple realized that if the marriage must work, if you must have a better marriage, then it is the responsibility of each partner in the marriage to make him or herself a better partner, a better person, a better human being.

The man or woman in every marriage relationship must resolve to be a better person. He or she must take time out to identify his or her weaknesses that have continuously put a strain on the marriage. And once these weaknesses have been identified then, the person must make an effort to get rid of them.

Before I got married I didn't really know much about my level of patience, may be because it had not been tested. After I got married, I discovered I had become impatient with my wife. I always wanted something to be done quickly and now. And when this was not done in the time I wanted, I complained to her and sometimes over and over again about her inability to do what I told her or expected her to do.

I continued this attitude for quite a while, until it dawned on me that I was being impatient with her and that I needed to change. I started training myself to be patient with her, no matter the delays I would always allow room for more time and at best I would remind and encourage her to do what we have set to do together if she was slowing down on her part.

This has made me a better person. I have learnt to be patient with my kids, workers, friends and other people. I have continued to work on my patience and I personally can see outstanding results.

For any marriage to work and flourish both people involved in the marriage relationship must continue to strive to be better persons and together they will become better couples.

Key 5: Love Your Spouse

Love is a complex word that cannot be narrowed down to likeness and sexual desires for a person. To understand love in full, we need to put it into the context of its expression. Love can be expressed in four major ways or forms or styles which includes:

i. Phileo Love

This type of love refers to an affectionate, warm and tender love that does not involve sex. It makes you desire friendship with someone. It is love in the noun form. It is how you feel about someone. It is a committed and chosen love.

ii. Storge Love

This is love for family and friends. It is the kind of love that parents naturally feel for their children; the love that family members have for each other; or the love that friends feel for each other.

Sometimes this friendship love may turn into a romantic relationship, and the couple in such a relationship becomes best friends. Storge love is unconditional, accepts flaws or faults and ultimately drives you to forgive. It's committed, sacrificial and makes you feel secure, comfortable and safe.

iii. Eros

This is the most glamourized type of love. You see it everywhere on television, internet, social media, bill boards, newspapers etc. Eros is a passionate and intense love that arouses romantic feelings; it is the kind that often triggers "high" feelings in a new relationship and makes you say the words - I love you. It is simply an emotional and sexual love.

This type of romantic love must be managed properly at the beginning of every relationship that is intended to culminate in marriage.

It stirs up a very strong desire for sex which seeks expression for satisfaction and if self control is not applied, it leads to unwanted sex, then unexpected pregnancy followed by the shame of having a child outside wedlock.

Eros love can be selfish, because it focuses more on self instead of on the other person. If one partner "in love" does not feel good about the relationship anymore, they will stop loving each other.

iv. Agape

This is an unconditional love that sees beyond the outer surface and accepts the recipient for whom he or she is, regardless of their flaws, shortcomings or faults. It's the type of love that everyone strives to have for their fellow human beings. Even if you don't like someone, you decide to love them just as a human being. It is a type of love that is all about sacrifice as well as giving and expecting nothing in return. it is love demonstrated by one's behaviour towards another person. It is a committed and chosen love.

Marriage is not a fling. It is not just a boy meeting girl relationship that is mostly driven by physical attraction, heightened passion and sex. Though these are important but are only a small part of the equation to have a successful marriage.

Every marriage must have Phileo, Storge, Eros and Agape love all working together to strengthen and establish the marriage relationship.

The husband and wife in a marriage must be affectionate, warm and tender to each other. They must develop genuine feelings of care for one another, with each person looking after the needs of the other. They must both treat themselves kindly and not be harsh in anyway. They must remain committed towards the welfare of the other.

The love between a couple should be unconditional. They must accept the flaws of each other and be willing to forgive themselves. One of the grave dangers of marriages is when a couple refuse to forgive itself for hurts done to each other and keep throwing it up when the next quarrel happens.

Some spouses have even gone to the extreme of recording the faults or offences of their partners in a book or a recorder. This is terrible and would certainly make the marriage head for the rocks.

Even when they don't go to the extreme, some couples refuse to forgive their spouses which makes them refuse to give the best to the marriage thereby causing it to derail.

No matter how much sex has been abused in the world today, it still remains a very vital part of what makes a marriage successful.

Couples must remain passionate and find themselves attractive to one another. Sex must not be sidelined but made an integral part of the continuous bonding process that must take place to have a successful marriage.

Couples must continue to express that passion physically in sex as well as in words by continuously saying the words "I love you" and as well as in actions by giving themselves to their partners.

Selfishness must be put out of the way completely and the romance in a marriage must never be allowed to die.

Agape love is the most important component of a successful marriage. Each partner must accept the recipient for whom he or she is, regardless of their flaws, shortcomings or faults.

They can encourage themselves to change obvious weak behaviours that can derail the relationship, but they must not focus on fault finding and fault picking on each other.

A successful marriage is based on continuous sacrifices, the couple must focus on giving to each other without expecting anything in return except the same kind of love, affection and sacrifice from their spouse.

One of the things that has made us progress in our marriage despite the challenges is the basis of love.

We work on Agape love. We both know that love is being kind hearted to one another and we make effort to treat ourselves with care and respect. The easiest thing to do in a marriage is to take each other for granted because you have become very familiar with one another.

Since you know the weakness of your spouse and there is the tendency to try to use this against him or her. Try to avoid this as much as possible.

Another attribute of agape love we put into practice is patience. Nobody is born with patience; you have to train yourself to be a patient person.

Some people have developed extra ordinary patience based on the circumstances life has dealt them. Because we know we are not perfect and have weaknesses, we have over time trained ourselves with one another.

We also know that agape love does not keep records of wrongs and we try to live on that principle. Even though sometimes we have found ourselves blaming each other for being responsible for our present predicaments, we soon quickly retrace our steps and apologize.

Agape love is not rude, arrogant or proud. Talking to each other with respect is vital to the survival of any marriage. If couples are always tongue lashing each other, it is the fastest way to destroy a marriage. Negative words can hurt like fire and leave deep burnt scars on the soul and spirits of the receiver. If used consistently, they become the reality of the marriage.

I have found myself many times tongue lashing my wife because of my emotional outburst. And when I am done with it, most times I feel very bad and have to make a series of apologies to my hurt wife. We heal and become better.

We also do not let pride get in the way. It is funny, but, pride can exist between a couple. This can be as a result of one partner coming from a privileged background than the other, if care is not taken the partner will always use that against the other, making it seem that he or she is doing the other a favour by getting married to them. It can also swing the other way when the partner from the less privileged home continues to accuse the other of using the family background to intimidate him or her. In my home, we are fortunate that our both parents are from the middle class, but even at that I always caution myself when I begin to see myself more superior to my wife as a man and with that in mind refuse to do jobs in the home for which I can be of help to her.

Agape love is not selfish. Selfishness is simply thinking what suits you and not giving adequate concern on what the other partner wants. If any spouse is selfish in the marriage it will generate lots of frictions. The marriage that works is the one that is always looking to the need of the other partner. This we try to practice in our marriage and it has helped us greatly.

For any marriage to be successful LOVE must be at its core, anything other than that will lead to its eminent collapse.

Key 6: No Third Party

Before people get married, they have developed strong bonds with either their parents, siblings or sometimes their friends. Sometimes these bonds are so deep such that the individual shares everything with the person or that close relative.

These previous relationships do not disappear just because the person involved is now married. Most of the times the relationship a spouse had with that close relative continues a long time even after marriage, and that is where the problem lies.

If the spouse who has built that external relationship fails to realize that he or she is a now in a new legal, spiritual, mental and deeply emotional relationship, that requires privacy and needs to be protected, he or she may innocently continue to divulge every information, activity and issues that happen in the home to that close confidant who is now a third party.

If the close confidant is selfish, immature or does not have the best interest of the marriage at heart, he or she may continue to give counsel that will stir up strife within the couple and may eventually lead to its dissolution.

There are so many marriages today that have been broken due to wrong actions taken based on wrong advice given by a third party.

The dread for "Mother-In-Laws", stem from this third party influence. The wife in marriage is often weary, afraid, careful and sometimes cynical about the mother of her husband, based on all the stories she had heard of the influence of mother-in-laws on their sons.

With this mentality, the attitude of the wife going into the marriage is more of confrontation than getting along with the mother of her husband.

And this swings both ways. The mother-in-law herself, not coming to grasp that her son is now married, will still want to maintain that strong bond she has built with her son over the years, and will see any other person taking attention from her as an intruder that includes her son's wife.

This "tit for tat" relationship can go on between the wife and mother-in-law for a very long time, if a decisive stop is not put to it by the couple.

Every couple in a marriage must as matter of principle, reduce to the barest minimum the influence of a third party on their marriage.

They must realize that their interest as a couple comes first before any external considerations. If they make this a basis for their marriage, they will seek to resolve issues that arise amongst themselves without getting a third party involved.

That is not to say that, when couples are experiencing serious challenges in their marriage, they cannot seek for help.

If help is needed it should be sought for, either together as a couple or from those close confidants who are matured, have the couple's interests at heart and have some experience in helping couples get along with their marriage issues.

I made that a priority in my marriage after seeing the damage third parties did to my parent's relationship. They were so many issues thrown up in the course of their marriage that were influenced by third party suggestions, advice and influence.

These led to so many fights, that I resolved in my own marriage that no matter what it takes, I will not allow any third party into my home and agreed with my wife from the onset, to make every effort to solve our challenges internally. And this has served us well.

Key 7: Agreement – Have the Same Mind

Can two persons walk together when they agree-absolutely not? Two people with different mindsets, education, friends and from different background and environment, who both think differently, cannot successfully work together except if they have a basis of agreement.

Their minds are far on both ends of the line. For any marriage to succeed, the couple must have to be the on the same page on fundamental issues that form the basis of their marriage.

They must agree from the first day of their marriage on how they will approach, deal with and respond to issues that confront every marriage. Such issues include:

o **Finances:** How the family will make money, how will the money be managed, what is required daily, weekly and monthly by the family, is there an investment strategy for the home, how does the couple handle external requests from parents and siblings etc.

o **Relationship with Family and Friends**: They have to agree on how to relate with parents and siblings of both couples e.g. what level of access will they be given into the affairs and activities of the home. Will it be a general access or based on the character and disposition of each parent, sibling or relative?

The couple must also agree which of their friends as singles will be upgraded as family friends and which will they have to gradually let go, based on sincere and deep analysis of character, perception and reality of these individuals. They must also determine what kind of new friends they want to make and how many.

o **Where to Live:** The couple must agree in what kind of neighbourhood, they want to live and want their children to grow up in, based on the mindset of the people, opportunities available, access to schools, hospitals and some other basic amenities of life. They have to agree to work hard and move to a place they want to live if they are not currently in that place yet.

o **Career Pursuits:** They must also agree of which career to pursue individually and collectively based on the dreams and aspirations of each of them, sacrifices that must be made to achieve this, and its overall benefits to the family. In today's very fast and busy world, both of them must work to make both ends meet, it is important they choose careers that will give them time to attend to their marriage and children. For example a couple who both are medical doctors, which is a very busy professional job, may find it difficult to give time to themselves and their children. If this is the case, the couple must set out time for purposeful vacations where they will have enough time for themselves and the kids which they may not have normally.

If the couple has a choice, the woman can decide to take ups jobs such teaching or lecturing that will give her adequate time to attend to the family while the man can pursue his dreams. After a while, when the children are grown up, she can continue the pursuit of her own dreams. This is what transpired in my marriage. When we got married, my wife was still in school, while I had just started out my own business.

By the grace of God it grew and the business was able to take care of both of us and the family. She was able to stay at home and nurture the children. They have grown up well to be very responsible. When the business slowed down, it was time for my wife to pursue her long cherished dream of being a broadcaster and that is where we are today.

Key 8: Love With Your Words

The words "I Love You" is one of the easiest words for a woman to say and one of the most difficult for a man to utter. I can relate with this from my own marriage experience.

My wife is always expressing her love for me and she says "I Love You" over and over and over again, and I times wonder whether she doesn't get tired of saying it.

She can wake up in the morning, give me a kiss and say the words "I Love You", only for me to say I love you too. Most of the times she is always the first to do so. She continually sends me text messages, calls me just to tell me the same words.

During courtship, when I was trying to woo her, I found myself saying those words frequently, on phone, when we were together or on a date. But when we got married, I slowed considerably on this and she always complained about it.

Words are the materials for the mind and the human spirit. When a person is exposed to a continuous flow of negative words they injure the soul and can damage the human spirit. Also, when a person is exposed to a continuous flow of positive words that individual is encouraged, strengthened and emboldened.

Just as negative words and positive words have their influence, no words at all also have their own influence.

Everybody knows that if you leave a land bare without planting any seeds, weeds will grow. The same applies to the human mind and in this case the **"marriage-mind"**. If no loving words are continuously expressed and exchanged between the couple, other unsolicited information which is usually most times negative, will feed the mind of the marriage and will cause weeds – friction, suspicions, misinformation and misunderstanding to breed.

And if this continues for a long time, the marriage will begin to experience cracks. And in cracks is where all kinds of insects and little reptiles reside. This means the cracks that open up in marriage will become a breeding ground for more trouble if it is not checked.

Couples must make frantic effort to continue to express love to each other with words. The words "I love you" must be used at every given opportunity.

The world out there is a hostile place. The man or woman who must go outside to work is exposed to the challenges and daily grinds of life. He or she will be confronted, challenged, sidelined, stepped on, cheated or insulted by colleagues, associates, the boss in the office or in the bus on the way back home or any other place within the course of a working day.

When that individual gets home, all ruffled up from the hassles of the day, he or she must be able to come into the warm embrace of a loving spouse who encourages him or her with words saying I am still with you no matter what the world says.

This gives strength and emboldens the husband or wife to go out and try again, full of hope and life.

But, if after all these, that individual comes home, and there are no words to encourage, build and strengthen or at worse, negative words are spoken, then pressure of the tension already bottled up from outside, will be heightened and may eventually explode which results in quarrels, fights and insults.

Words are powerful, especially, when spoken from a loving spouse.

Key 9: Express Displeasure Lovingly

In the previous key, we discussed at length the power of words being used to encourage, build and strengthen the marriage.

One thing that will be obvious in any marriage relationship is the weaknesses of both couples.

A spouse will easily see what the other is struggling with and has a duty to help his or her partner come out of it or cover up the obvious weakness in their marriage. In marriage it is almost impossible to hide your flaws from your spouse and in times of challenges, it is easy to use those flaws to attack your spouse.

A marriage is made up of two imperfect beings. And because they are imperfect, they are subject to continuous mistakes which may not be revealed to each other before marriage. Such weaknesses which could be in talking too much, spending too much time with friends rather than with spouse, been carefree with money, snoring when sleeping, eating too much and so many others, may not be a problem when the couple where singles, but can become a serious concern when they are married.

In my case, I later discovered I could be very bossy. At the time I got married, I had my own company, with employees who I daily issued instructions to get the job done. Early in my marriage I took that same disposition home, and began to give orders to my wife.

Most times she would lovingly tell me that I am not in the office and she was not an employee working in my company, and advised me to change my tone and approach when talking to her, at other times she will get angry with me.

In my search for knowledge, I read Myles Munroe's book about marriage, in it he advises couples when coming home to drop their "Office Mode" – the mode of being the boss and take on the "Home Mode" when they change to become the loving husband or the submissive wife. This helped me a great deal to change my attitude as soon as I got home.

Another factor that influenced my life in marriage was my parents. While growing up, I had watched my dad who was a military man, giving orders in the house which everyone including my mum was obliged to follow, I had in my mind the idea that one of a man's job was to give orders around the home.

So, even when I was not influenced by the "Office Mode" I exhibited what I had learnt from my parents in marriage and of course, my wife didn't like a bit of it.

The point here is that couples will have challenges with the weaknesses of their spouse, it may even get to the point of irritation, but it is the responsibility of both of them not to ignore these weaknesses but to work to change to it.

This should be done in the most loving way possible. The partner who really feels uncomfortable about the conduct, actions or character exhibited by his or her spouse, must choose his or her words carefully when expressing such concern, so that the other spouse does not feel embarrassed, derided or humiliated.

It must be done in a time and atmosphere of love and not at the point of heated verbal exchanged or when the spouse is angry and the atmosphere is tensed up. If this is done consistently, then, it will help to build a strong marriage.

Key 10: Leave The Past Behind

Leaving the past behind and reaching out for the future is one of the biggest secrets of success in life.

The past holds nothing but memories. It has included in it mistakes, hurts, regrets, past relationships and everything else that belongs to the past.

The past can never be changed or reversed; it is gone forever into the annals of history. If it is continuosly rehashed it will be of little benefit.

The only serious benefit of the past is that it provides us a hindsight view of what we would have done better and gives us the opportunity to correct and amend our ways and actions in future. It provides us with a rich reservoir of experience that we can learn from and helps us to make better choices going forward.

Any individual, who holds on the past, will not go into the future. He or she will want the "Good Old

Days" to come back and the reality is that, this won't happen.

If you relive the past you may get angry at yourself, in fact very angry on what you should have or should not have done if you knew what you know now. But, the truth is that you had to go through those mistakes, hurts, disappointments and pains because it was a moment of training for you, which though at that time was very painful, but have provided you with pearls of wisdom you would not have known in any other way, but, to go through.

As individuals have past, so do couples have a past. From the start, which most times is rocky, when the couples are just starting out, lots of mistakes will be made by both partners.

There will be carried over idiosyncrasies from the single life that will have both positive and negative consequences.

An individual who has a stingy approach to money as a single will definitely carry this over to the marriage. He or she will find it very difficult to purchase items that will give a little comfort to the home. E.g. when one spouse is marking his or her birthday, such an individual may find extremely difficult to buy his spouse a gift because of the mentality of thriftiness and this will definitely infuriate his or her spouse.

This disposition will certainly make the couples miss opportunities that they would have invested in and made their financial lives better, but because of stinginess those opportunities were missed.

Though after some years of being married, with the blending and learning that goes with it, such a spouse would have changed, but the remembrance of missed financial opportunities will continue to be a source of pain to the couple.

If the affected couple is always reminded of what he or she did, it will be a source of tension, quarrels and fights.

Reminders of the past will not help the marriage. The couple must realize that the past is gone, and that errors or mistakes were made because of ignorance, lack of knowledge or inexperience.

It is time to move forward, take the wisdom learnt and make progress.

3. Conclusion

No matter the number of marriages we have seen fail in society, which is constantly on the increase, marriage still remains a beautiful relationship that should last for a lifetime if couples walk on the right principles.

The principles of Companionship, Growing Together, Love, Restricting Third Party Influence, Leaving the Past Behind and others that have been discussed in this book and hopefully other principles you will find in your quest for learning, will help you achieve the desired happy marriage you have so much dreamed off.

The lessons learnt from this book are for us all to persevere and hold on to what we believe in, no matter the oppositions, hurdles and challenges.

After many years down the line our love is still growing stronger and stronger. This can also be your Story.

Keep learning, keep growing and have a wonderful marriage.

God Bless You the Unmarried and Married.

ABOUT THE AUTHOR

Mr. Vincent Hope Okoh is a graduate of Mathematics Education and a very experienced Educator with over twenty (20) years of Teaching, Instructing and Training Experience.

He is an author of several academic and non-academic books among which are "My Leadership Collections", "The Aisle", "The Story of My Mother", "Deeper Secrets of Wealth" etc.

He is an Entrepreneur, Management Expert and Leader, having lead his own company from an unknown position to an ICT firm of repute that has trained so many individuals in various ICT Skills, who are currently employed in different sectors of the economy.

He is happily married to Mrs. Deborah Nanchin Vincent and they are blessed with three beautiful daughters Angel, Joy and Anita.